Ethics of Luxury

materialism and imagination

for Christos & Sophie
/ Ihor
Jan 08

BY

JEANNE RANDOLPH

AFTERWORD AND IMAGE SELECTION

BY IHOR HOLUBIZKY

2007

Co-published with Plug In ICA
/Plug In Editions, Winnipeg

Library and Archives Canada
Cataloguing in Publication

Randolph, Jeanne, 1943-
    Ethics of luxury : materialism and
imagination / by Jeanne Randolph ;
introduction by Anthony Kiendl ; afterword
by Ihor Holubizky.

Includes bibliographical references.
ISBN 978-0-920397-46-6

    1. Luxury. 2. Consumption (Economics)—
Moral and ethical aspects. 3. Consumption
(Economics) in art. 4. Wealth—Moral and
ethical aspects. I. Title.

BT1535.L9R35 2007   178   C2007-902431-9

Editor: Ihor Holubizky
Managing Editor: Robert Labossiere
Publishing Interns: Jane van Keerbergen,
Rachael Pleet
Printed in Canada by Marquis

Graphic Design: Susan Chafe
This book was typeset in the fonts:
Hoefler Text and *The Mix*

YYZBOOKS is represented by the Literary Press
Group of Canada www.lpg.ca and distributed
by LitDistCo orders@litdistco.ca

YYZBOOKS is dedicated to publishing critical
writings on Canadian art and culture.
YYZBOOKS is the publishing programme of
YYZ Artists' Outlet, an artist-run centre that
presents challenging programs of visual art,
film, video, performance, lectures, and
publications. YYZ Artists' Outlet is supported by
its members, The Canada Council for the Arts,
the Ontario Arts Council, and the City of Toronto
through the Toronto Arts Council.

YYZBOOKS

140 – 401 Richmond Street W
Toronto ON   M5V 3A8   Canada

PLUG IN
iCa

We are grateful for the support of Plug In ICA/
Plug In Editions, Winnipeg. Plug In ICA is a
laboratory for research and a nexus for the
presentation of art that confronts ideas and
issues affecting today's society, and interdis-
ciplinary projects spanning architecture, film,
television, photography, sound, and new media.
Plug In ICA acknowledges the support of the
Manitoba Arts Council, Canada Council for
the Arts, Winnipeg Arts Council, the Winnipeg
Foundation, the Department of Canadian
Heritage, the WH and SE Loewen Foundation,
Investors Group, CanWest Global Commun-
ications, our donors, patrons and volunteers.

 Canada Council   Conseil des Arts
for the Arts   du Canada

YYZ Artists' Outlet and YYZBOOKS gratefully
acknowledge the support of The Canada Council
for the Arts and the Paul D. Fleck Fellowship for
2003 in making this book possible.

Note from the publisher: Every reasonable effort has been made to contact the holders of copyright
for images and texts reproduced in this book. The publishers will gladly receive information that will
enable errors or omissions to be rectified in subsequent editions.

CONTENTS

Ryan Arnott [b. Canada, 1952]
Untitled (Lead Diamond) 1989
Lead, 4.3 x 6.2 x 6.2 cm
Collection of the Art Gallery of Hamilton
Courtesy of the artist

P R E A M B L E

> Life had poured
> more than sufficient. How could we ever be cheated,
> ever betrayed, we with every reward
> over-rewarded?[1]

There are millions of North Americans whose lives, compared to the majority of humans on Earth, are materially "over-rewarded." For me this fact dramatizes and stabilizes a meaning for North American luxury. This meaning quivers in my mind like a bird in a flame. Everyone with a conscience wishes for a remedy to poverty. But apparently pure guilt is not a good enough impetus for redistribution of the wealth. No one knows what remedies are good enough. Remedy is not the motive of this essay. I am writing this because in so many ways it seems as if life in enclaves of luxury continues the delusion of an ethics of scarcity. In the shadow of the twentieth-century slogan "Just do it," I worry that collective understanding has been stilled and personal imagination coagulated. It is still better to think (while not knowing what to do) than to stop thinking. Thought is all I have to contribute. Overwhelmed as we are, we are still free to think ethically about our luxury.

1 Rainer Maria Rilke, Selected Poems, *"Meaningful Word, 'Inclination,'"*
   trans., intro. J. B. Leeshman (Hammondsworth: Penguin, 1964) p 31

Iain Baxter& [b. England 1936, Lives in Canada]
Fruit Crates, Okanagan Valley, British Columbia, 1965
Duratran light box, 68.5 x 46 x 14 cm
Courtesy of the artist and Corkin Gallery, Toronto

The value—also the vulnerability—of any thought resides in this necessity of public and personal sustenance in consciousness and in conversation.

I am keeping in mind also, corollary to these reflections on ethical imagining, that among the many intangibles valued and sustained in enclaves of luxury, there is a companion to imagining. In fellowship with imagining one will find reason, the practice of reasoning.

Reasoning is not the opposite of imagining. Wherever dilemmas occur, both reasoning and imagining will be rallied to understand them. Reasoning and imagining are inextricable in the interpretation of day-to-day predicaments. It strikes me as misleading to explore imagination as if the essence of it never mingles with reason. The practice of imagining and the practice of reasoning are an ordinary admixture. I highlight this point only in passing yet, in a sense, if reason is vulnerable to devaluation, imagination is not inherently exempt. Or vice versa. And reasoning is vulnerable to devaluation: not only is reasoning assailed by the same old forms of fundamentalism that Spinoza abhorred (and the same old snootiness bemoaned by John Kenneth Galbraith), but also, since the twentieth century, the first century of the Era of Advertising, reasoning is assailed by unique rhetorical charms:

Cherry. Strawberry. Grape.
Three reasons to buy Froot-Loops™

This is not funny. Not to me. Reification would only be amusing
if contemporary North American society were peopled
predominantly by philosophers. Philosophers have a natural
immunity to literal thinking. But there are many different
ways of being and being beneficial to each other without
turning into philosophers. And we don't have to become
philosophers to discuss our society's continued reliance upon
reasoning. Reification (which jeopardizes both reason and
imagination) will not be funny when it is the rule, and especially
not when it is the rule of commodity adoration, a rule that

> ...clogs men's minds with dogmatic formulas, that leave
> no room for sound reason, not even enough room to
> doubt with.[2]

Isn't it at least worth a sigh of "Yo! Awesome Dudes!" that
some groups of people will work to maintain the experience
of reason: reason as the name of a way of thinking that has

2 The Philosophy of Spinoza: selected from his chief works, *ed. with
   intro. Joseph Ratner (New York: The Modern Library, 1927) p 6*

taken many thousands of years and many thousands of conversations in many thousands of communities to conjure, to practice, to verify and to teach.

Reason once was social always; it began in conversation, in the dialogues between curious humans. It was cultivated and it now flourishes in a myriad of forms, including the forms of our day, including the form promoted by the institutions of advertising: "a justification."[3]

It is not the term *reason* whose traditional definition I insist must never be abandoned. The term is mutable and mortal. I am considering how a group, a community, a society, sustains the possibility of practicing what it recognizes as reason, call it what we will.

Regarding this I am addressing those of us who live in enclaves of luxury. At present we apparently admire people who deliberately enhance the practice of reasoning. We admire people dedicated to the exercise of reason and still I fret whether we are taking the capacity to reason for granted

3 The Random House Dictionary of the English Language, *second edition [unabridged] 1987, p 1608*

while consumerism and the institutions such as advertising that promote consumerism, proceed unimpeded to obfuscate reasoning's value.

In enclaves of luxury at times it seems that the practice of reasoning is delegated predominantly to scientists. But scientists have a specialized method of reasoning. The rest of us have a millenniums-long tradition of reasoning that is inextricable not only from conversation but also from imagining and ethics.

Maybe some people are wishing and waiting for scientific reasoning itself to guide the way, anticipating that nothing will go awry as long as the value of imagination can be enriched by meticulous scientific exploration, or by strict analyses of its salutary consequences. If scientists are committed to gathering evidence that imagination is vital to our existence, we need them to continue, but here, for now, I am venturing further into the question of ethics and luxury. What I am writing here is based on reasoning, but not with the scientific method. I make a point of offering an imprecise picture. Definitions that might be subject to experiment and quantification add value, but I am trying to profess another kind of value as

James Angus [b. 1970, Australia. Lives in New York]
Installation view of Rio Phase Shift, 2003;
White birch mahogany, basswood, plywood, mdf; 190 x 140 x 170 cm
Untitled, 2003
Vinyl tape; 365 x 847 cm
At Gavin Brown's Enterprise, New York, February 12—March 6, 2004.
Courtesy of the artist and Roslyn Oxley9 Gallery, Sydney.

well. I am venturing, cheered on by *the Ethica Nichomachea* in which Aristotle said, "Precision is perhaps something more labourious than our purposes require."[4]

> "Is it even always an advantage to replace an indistinct picture by a sharp one? Isn't the indistinct one often exactly what we need?"[5]

I live in an enclave of luxury and I see materialism's effects here amidst intangible as well as tangible abundance. These effects are clearest to me when I observe materialist advertising's involvement in reasoning, in imagining and in the depiction of personal relationships. In contemplating this, my method will be, you might say, to make a hypothesis: "Ethical imagining can become a practice in everyday life." To comprehend the changes in human relations, in reason and in culture that evolved with twentieth century materialism I am invoking the relevance of an ethical imagination that is vaguely human, not an objectively perceived phenomenon. With no wish for precision, I am invoking an idea of ethical imagining, but without hope of quantifying its effects. I am invoking "ethical imagining" as an illusion sustained by a community, and maintained as a cultural practice.

4 *(Chicago: Great Books Foundation, undated) p 2*
5 *Ludwig Wittgenstein*, Philosophical Investigations, *number 71, trans. E.M. Anscombe (Oxford: Basil Blackwell, 1953)*.

I am guessing that ethics are evoked by reasoning, imagining and empathy, and I am alarmed at the vulnerability of reason, imagination and empathy under the influence of materialism and its toady, advertising. Empathy is a serious matter. I acknowledge this and am incapable of discussing it further. Empathy is an essential aspect of personal and social living that requires much more than is implied by this, my brief inkling of ethical imagination.

For now, because the psychoanalytic interpretation of culture is where I trust there is hope, I am mentioning reason and emphasizing imagination. I am, in passing, implicating reason because it is an intangible practice (albeit with intensively material consequences). Reason could utterly calcify into mere literal thinking unless it is socially cultivated. Yet I also claim that in everyday consciousness (and in this essay) the practices of imagining and reasoning need not always be defined, refined and compartmentalized.

The value of reasoning (and the value of an idea such as ethical imagining)—and hence its vulnerability—depends on its social sustenance, its maintenance as illusory experiences valuable enough to be considered real. I will continue as if an idea of ethical imagining is a valuable illusory experience rather than a valuable commodity.

I began these reflections in earnest several years ago when I snipped a picture from the local real estate pages. The caption read 'You've only got one life to live.' A girl, photographed in her minimal, crinkly bathing suit, sits on the edge of a condo swimming pool. She is tiny. Her forearms compare to the stems of tulips. The girl's repose elongates her legs bent at thigh sloping up to the crook of the flexed knees, and down again to her ankles, down to the petite red endpoints of her polished toenails. The girl's narrow torso is turned slightly toward me, her breasts swivelling behind the stiff skimpy top of her suit, a fish belly white suit overlain with green octopi tumbling with silver sea horses in a profusion of lavender grasses. The pale ochre patio deck is the texture of the finest sandpaper. The smooth wide rim of the pool is glacial white. Turquoise water laps lightly against the citrine wall. Golden highlights accent this young lady's bronze hair pulled back from her wide, unfurrowed brow. Black mascara cuts a silhouette through the blank sunlight. Her smile insinuates something I can't quite fathom.

She appears to be living in an enclave of material luxury.
I too am living in an enclave of material luxury. The enclave
where I live is in Canada. In this enclave, and there are many
others, my days are decorated, cluttered, convenienced,
inconvenienced and jam-packed by physical objects useful
and useless, amusing and confusing, elegant and ugly, durable
and disintegrating, each and everything pregnant with qualities
for which there are thousands of adjectives in the English
language. Thousands of objects are poured into this enclave of
luxury, thousands of goods and commodities made incarnate
by industrialized means, by artisanal efforts, by labours of love
and by slave labour too, by traditional means, and also by
idiosyncratic methods, in a myriad of media, compounding
into an avalanche of things made of animal, vegetable, mineral,
polymer, telecommunication and all possible amalgams of
these. In the enclave of luxury where I live, as in other North
American enclaves, nothing stops the avalanche of commodities
and commercial images of commodities.

Like the suspect smoke of hot tobacco in the pipe clenched
between my teeth, my irritated ideas waft in shapeless
currents, traceless after collision with solid objects. And there
are so many solid and semi-solid objects. Shapeless smoke
and ideas slither against them, sometimes encircle them,
rarely encompass them fully. The objects are relentless, like a
contagion that doesn't always travel under the same name,
although the name that is said is consumerism.

There is not enough interval between one object and the next
to associate one or the other with a time, a place, a likeness
to, or a difference from memories of other times and places;
no room to see a story form in the sequence of things, or to
consider this object or that as simile.

After dark in the enclave, the deep pile wall-to-wall commodities threaten to outnumber the twinklings in the celestial nightscape: if my neighbour, a bank teller, could imagine 400,000 asteroids, will she comprehend these in terms of fifty-dollar bills? Do the accountants for Goodyear® find the phrase "3,000,000,000,000,000 stars" an ordinary number in terms of rubber tires? My friend the shoe store salesclerk surely wouldn't think of "2,000 galaxies" as a reminder of his inventory.

> ...Life had poured
> more than sufficient. How could we ever be cheated,
> ever betrayed, we with every reward
> over-rewarded?

This fragment of poetry is a good-enough depiction of the enclave of luxury where I have lived all my life, even though in my life I have lived in five different North American megapoli.

Canada includes enclaves of luxury, and Benedict Spinoza
would have pronounced them good because these enclaves

> have freed every man from fear, that he may live in all
> possible security; in other words, to strengthen his
> natural right to exist and work without injury to himself
> or other... [6]

The Canadian-born economist John Kenneth Galbraith has
also described a "more than sufficient," and obviously
attainable enclave of luxury:

> Exemption from manual toil; escape from boredom
> and confining and severe routine; the chance to
> spend one's life in clean and physically comfortable
> surroundings; and some opportunity for applying
> one's thought to the day's work.[7]

6 The Philosophy of Spinoza: Selected from His Chief Works, *ed. Joseph
   Ratner (New York: The Modern Library, 1927) p 335*

7 The Affluent Society *(Boston: New American Library, 1958) p 267*

Somewhere or in some sense between Spinoza's threatened life in the mid 1600s[8] and the over-rewarded life in enclaves of luxury in the mid 1900s, living conditions more than sufficient for physical survival became attainable by the millions.

Galbraith's economic analysis also took due notice of the ever-escalating judgment "regarding the minimum for decency,"[9] an ever-excusable criterion for lording it over someone(s) else. This was Galbraith's acknowledgment of our innate propensity to establish hierarchies. Our primate tendency to maintain hierarchies can impel finer and finer distinctions, and it is to be expected that having certain consumer goods, for instance, may become less a badge of shared affluence in an enclave of luxury and more the mark of relative decency (This was perfectly demonstrated by the now infamous General Motors car dealers' ad in Vancouver newspapers, in which, in 2003, public transit buses were depicted as infested with "CREEPS AND WEIRDOS."). The apparent relativity of luxury cannot be extricated from the sociology of communities.

This has to be acknowledged; yet whatever I am writing here it is not sociology.

8 *Spinoza's mentor Jan de Witt and de Witt's brother were murdered by a Christian mob; other associates were burned at the stake.*
9 *Galbraith, p. 251*

Iain Baxter&
Sign, Highway 17, near Sudbury, Ontario, 1969
Duratran light box, 91.5 x 122 x 14 cm
Courtesy of the artist and Corkin Gallery, Toronto

En passant, yet central to what I am writing, Galbraith noted "No one should suppose there is anything agreeable about the assumption of [one's] affluence."[10]

Amidst all the intellectual riches of Galbraith's *The Affluent Society*, I have plucked this fragment of psychology as a premonition about ethics in enclaves of luxury. Galbraith noted that there is a certain embarrassment to sitting pretty. What with luxury seeming relative, it might even feel somehow unrealistic to admit one really has quite enough already. In an enclave of luxury couldn't there always be more, more, more? And anyway isn't this what moral truisms ("Here in North America we are so fortunate.") are for, to account for the luxury, to get on with the business at hand, and to forget that "the mind depreciates what it finds easy to explain." [11]

Galbraith noticed this, and so have I: how unlikely it is to feel astonishment on a daily basis that one is living in an enclave of luxury.

10 *Galbraith, p 14*
11 *Augustine*, De Doctrina Christiana, *2.6.7 trans. D.W. Robertson Jr. [*On Christian Doctrine*] (Indianapolis: Bobbs-Merrill, 1958) cited in Christopher Kirwan*, Augustine, *(London: Routledge, 1991) p 13*

It seems to me it has become normal to lose one's reference point for good fortune and to fret instead about better. It seems unrealistic to accept that one is "over-rewarded." In a gated community, which is the example *par excellence* of an enclave of luxury, it seems risky to trust the good that you enjoy. "When the great fear of losing it hangs over you, there is no way you can be happy."[12]

For many of us in an enclave of luxury, whether within built gates or imagined entitlement, life is normal, so normal that a definition of luxury such as Spinoza's or Galbraith's could evoke plaintive singing,

> Is that all there is?
> Is that all there is?
> Is that all there is my friend... [13]

12 *Augustine*, De Moribus Ecclesiae Catholicae, *from Christopher Kirwan*, Augustine (*N.Y: Routledge, 1991) p 189*
13 *Lyrics and music by Peggy Lee*

Eugene Carchesio [b. Australia 1960]
D.N.E., 47 Songs Humans Shouldn't Sing, 1990
Record cover
Courtesy of the artist and Kindling Records, Brisbane

Is that all there is to luxury? In the seventeenth century it would have been obvious that's all there is. There are places on other continents where it is obvious now. There are desperate communities just outside our enclave where it is obvious.

On the other hand, I expect there will always be someone who forwards a more swank definition of luxury. It is true that most enclaves of luxury don't have the substance of royal estates. A regal life in any era of human existence proves how puny is the luxury of ninety-eight per cent of the rest of humanity; the pocketbook of a magnate or superstar belittles the hoard of "over-rewarded" earthlings, not to mention the holdings of unlucky ones. If the relativity of wealth has been the reality since time began, then, logically, luxury has no boundary: we need only compare ourselves to emperors and Formula One race car drivers to realize how modest are our greediest dreams.

With this logic as our roadmap, acknowledging how close to the legless nematode we are on the Great Chain of Being Rich, our economic conscience (admittedly an absurd kind of conscience to posit) comes to a standstill.

Braking the conscience, however, enhances nothing for a curious mind. The seemingly realistic logic of primate hierarchy merely hurries us along a never-ending detour from the muddy road of ethics. The seemingly realistic logic of the pecking order, analogous to the cliché "There will always be someone smarter and prettier," seems closer to the doctrine of predestination than to inventiveness and speculation. Yet, happily, living in an enclave of luxury, when someone insists that Spinoza's and Galbraith's definitions cannot possibly be all there is to luxury, we can afford to listen to and converse about their reasons.

I am toying with the idea that in an enclave of luxury, people might concede that their material circumstances are plentiful, indeed "over-rewarded." I am asking whether this recognition might provoke reconsideration of what luxury fully entails—reconsideration on the basis of intangible luxuries that material abundance has obscured.

DON'T WORRY
I'M
HARMLESS

Simon Poulter [b. England 1963]
Identity Card
Viral web project, 2003-05: www.viral.info, issued 14/11/03
Courtesy of the artist

Here we are, born into many assumptions, assumptions elevated to the status of working fictions, and sometimes exalted as unshakable beliefs. One of these assumptions is that "in a democracy" material wealth ensures the continuation of civilized practices.

What would be the social effect of scientific proof there is no link between material luxury and the husbandry of two of our most treasured civilized practices—reason and imagination? Suppose one day instead of announcing that a human infant had been successfully cloned, a "Human Belief Project" confirmed the practice of reason, or of imagination, is not directly correlated with material luxury? Would this information inspire people in enclaves of luxury to rethink their position? Or would we behold, in spite of what the late John Dewey hoped, that even in the presence of this new scientific intelligence:

> Prejudice, the pressure of immediate circumstance, self-interest and class interest, traditional customs,

institutions of accidental historic origin are not lacking, and they tend to take the place of intelligence.[14]

In his enclave of luxury Dewey must at times have felt very alone.

Suppose that we fully realized we are not living in a half-way house between normalcy and indecency. Suppose we fully recognized that we are actually living in an enclave of luxury. When should we start listing all the so-called civilized practices that give body to dreams of safety, dignity, justice, freedom, and laughter? Suppose a group of us (or all of us?) began to reconsider which intangible experiences we can afford to especially nourish because of this fact? Suppose "The Human Belief Project" encouraged us to cultivate our intangible luxuries above all? Would our society be secure in its civilized practices, knowing the value of intangibles supercedes those of materialism? We would certainly have a plenitude of intangibles to consider:

> reason, silliness, imagination, orthodoxy, generosity, curiosity, empathy, ingenuity, optimism, fairness, eccentricity, patience, bravery, honesty, absurdity,

14 *John Dewey,* Quest for Certainty, *Ch. X,* "*The Construction of Good*" *(G. P. Putnam's Sons, 1929) p 265*

lenience, dignity, skepticism, spontaneity, reputation, compromise, courtesy, reconciliation, learning, responsibility, friendship, gratitude, cooperation, selflessness, flexibility, thoroughness, playfulness, dedication, contemplation, resilience, versatility, compassion, organization, disorganization, precision, imprecision, bearing witness, care, elegance, ceremony, dissent, debate, peace, remembrance, attentiveness, leisure.

It is easier to forget intangibles than to list them all.

We may reconsider much, while not knowing what to do next.

I continue with these reflections about enclaves of luxury and ethics with no anticipation that what I am writing will be mistaken for advice.

CURRENTLY EXPERIENCING

VERY DISTRESSING

IDENTITY CRISIS

I'D LEAVE ME ALONE

IF I WAS YOU

Rowena Easton [b. England 1969]
Identity Card
Viral web project, 2003-05: www.viral.info, issued 18/11/03
Courtesy of the artist

In the history of philosophical ethics there has been a multiplicity of arguments for how to recognize good, what constitutes good behaviour, what constitutes good thought and what constitutes good character, with or without the assumption of god(s). Spinoza was very specific about a good life. A citizen would be free

> ...to refresh and restore himself in moderation with pleasant food and drink, with scents, with the beauty of green plants, with decoration, music, sports, the theater, and other things of this kind, which anyone can use without injury to another.[15]

Wouldn't a reasonable person agree that this is really living?

In 1953 the Cambridge philosopher G. E. Moore didn't find this description, or the entirety of Spinoza's *oeuvre* enough to go on.

15 Ethics, *Book IV, Proposition XLV, Corollary 2, Scholium*

We are all constantly in ordinary life asking such questions as: Would such and such a result be a good thing to bring about? Or would it be a bad thing? Would such and such an action be a right action to perform or would it be a wrong one? And what ethical philosophy tries to do is to classify all the different sorts of things which would be good or bad, right or wrong, in such a way as to be able to say: Nothing would be good, unless it had certain characteristics, or one or other of certain characteristics; and similarly nothing would be bad, unless it had certain properties or one or other of certain properties: and similarly with the question what sort of actions would be right, and what would be wrong.[16]

At that point also Moore offered his caveat. When a philosopher develops ethical ideas, there still remains

the question what is meant by saying that any proposition is true... And the question what are the different ways in which a proposition can be proved to be true; what are all the different sorts of reasons which are good reasons for believing anything? [17]

16 *G. E. Moore*, Some Main Problems In Philosophy, *Ch. I "What is Philosophy?" (London: George Allen and Unwin Ltd., 1953)*
17 *Moore, p 26*

1953 seems a long time ago.

Had the materialization of technological fantasies (a plethora of devices such as The Bomb, plastics, television, computers, antibiotics, etc.) changed philosophy?

Way before The Bomb the intelligentsia must have already expected scientists, not philosophers, to articulate how the universe holds together (and flies apart). If I had been a philosopher in the 1920s, believing that metaphysics is bunk, would I have turned to the one branch of philosophy kin to the scientific method, Logic? In those days, as in our own, massive power was institutionalized for purposes other than universal equality under the law or universal respite from the struggle for survival. Philosophy as a *poeisis*, insofar as it tackled ethics with Logic, became more and more disappointing. By the 1950s any philosophical career would have bumped its head on the low ceiling of logic: our entire world could actually explode during a Cold War; the time had ripened for domination by one of the most powerful instruments of public unreason ever—advertising.

Alan Flint [b. Canada 1958]
LOST 1996
Wood engraving, edition of 30, 26 x 56 cm
Courtesy of the artist

By the end of the twentieth century, as Mary Warnock noted in her 1971 edition of *Ethics Since 1900*,

> A new vocabulary of ethics is in the process of being developed.[18]

By 1994, the term ethics does not even appear in the index of the book *What Is Philosophy?* by Deleuze and Guattari, and yet the entire book sizzles with what we perceive as ethical fire. Deleuze and Guattari wrote within a web of civic and individual conscience that shivers whenever institutional powers desecrate human rights.

For many, including Deleuze and Guattari, when the Nazis brought the logic of technology into the service of mass murder, ethics could not be comprehended unless a marvelous imaginative practice was pulled into the foreground—the communal experience of complicity.

> It is not only our States but each of us, every democrat, who finds himself or herself not responsible for Nazism but sullied by it.[19]

18 *(Oxford: Oxford University Press, 1971) p 143*
19 *Trans. Hugh Tomlinson and Graham Burchell (New York: Columbia University Press, 1994) p 107*

Over-rewarded by mass media now "we are witnesses and this is the expression of our mode of belonging to the world."[20] It only takes a moment on-line to find

CATAGORIES: GO TO
Headlines, Hurricanes, Earthquakes,
Floods, Terrorism, Volcanoes
Bureau of Alcohol, Tobacco & Firearms
California Rescue Dog Association
Emotional Trauma Page

If you have visited a site with disaster related news please take a moment to share it with us!

20 *Gabriel Marcel*, The Philosophy of Existentialism, *trans.
Manya Harari (Secaucus N.J., Citadel Press, 1956) p 97*

EARTHQUAKES:
USGS Earthquake Hazards Program:
    Significant Earthquake Lists
This page is brought to you by the
    Earthquake Hazards Program URL:
    http://neic.usgs.gov/neis/eqlists/significant.html

LATEST QUAKES
Significant Earthquakes of the World
Earthquakes of magnitude 6.5 or greater or ones that
    caused fatalities, injuries or substantial damage
Significant Earthquakes of The United States,
    January 1986 - June 2005

We know we are witnesses, and we can sense viscerally what
complicity is, and yet   .

> It is clear that the normal development of a human being
> implies an increasingly precise and, as it were, automatic
> division between what concerns him and what does not,
> between things for which he is responsible and those for
> which he is not. Each one of us becomes the centre of a
> sort of mental space arranged in concentric zones of
> decreasing interest and participation.[21]

21 *Marcel, p 4*

François Dallegret [b. Morocco 1937, Lives in France and Canada].
Le Drug, Montreal (interior view), 1965
Photo: Bruno Massenet
© François Dallegret/SODRAC (2007)

A child's stuffed bunny scolds

> "You have downloaded the vole video without my
> permission!"

A Premier of Alberta tells reporters

> "Sit down and eat nothing but brains and spines for the
> rest of your life, then you might get mad cow disease."

Transubstantiation, as a third example, has been for centuries
a dramatic example of an unresolved paradox and opportunity
for gathering into a group on the basis of a shared imaginative
experience.

> "We can share a respect for illusory experience, and if we
> wish we may collect together and form a group on the
> basis of the similarity of our illusory experiences."[22]

22 *D. W. Winnicottt*, Playing and Reality *(Markham ON: Penguin, 1986) p 3*

I am asserting the very idea that the experience of "imagining" is an illusory experience. According to object relations psycho-analytic theory, imagination itself would be defined in the same terms as illusory experience. The texture of imagining comes from its provisionality. It is not necessarily beholden to the Reality Principle [23] nor is it always dominated by the Technological Ethos.[24]

23 *"One comes to learn a procedure by which, through a deliberate direction of one's sensory activities, and through suitable muscular action, one can differentiate between what is internal – what belongs to the ego – and what is external – what emanates from the outer world. In this way one makes the first step towards the introduction of the Reality Principle, which is to dominate future developments. This differentiation, of course, serves the practical purpose of enabling one to defend oneself." [Sigmund Freud,* Civilization and its Discontents, *trans. Joan Riviere, ed. James Strachey (London: Hogarth Press and the Institute of Psycho-Analysis, 1972) pp 4-5]*

24 *The Technological Ethos could be thought of as an ideology of quantification through which human experience is defined and perceived exclusively in terms of goals to be achieved. Technology will not concern itself with the experience of the subject, but instead with the materiality of the object. Technology's only reality is implementation in the active, literal sense. The Technological Ethos tends to diminish paradox, diminish subjectively distorted experience, and give no recognition to the impulse to interact with society for other than physical, social or economic self-defense. It is pervasive because everything we want requires some technique to obtain. The prevailing fantasy that arises out of the Technological Ethos, in which efficiency and objectivity are the supreme values, is the fantasy that any fact of life is worthwhile if it is precise enough, fast enough and powerful enough. [Jeanne Randolph,* Symbolization and Its Discontents, *ed. Steve Reinke (Toronto: YYZBOOKS, 1997) pp 69-70 and 72]*

Imagination is not obligated to let practicalities dominate, nor to judge itself in terms of dualistic language (true vs. untrue; reality vs. fantasy; possible vs. impossible; good vs. evil, etc.) The paradox of imagination is that it cannot imagine itself while it is experienced and it can't judge itself while experienced.

"I promise never to imagine cutting a kitten's throat" is a ridiculous proposition. Most of us wish that people would not get pleasure imagining such things to the exclusion of anything else. Even so, imagining *per se* leaves no traces, while planning may do so and performing always does. Imagining leaves no traces, which is not the same as saying imagining has no effect.

Imagining takes place in a zone of experience across which it becomes gradually indistinguishable from art. In the zone of art there is always imagined experience. Depictions by artists (explicitly or implicitly) present, like a magnifying glass, a virtual version of something. Between the polarities from material to abstract, between the thing and the idea, art revises phenomena without losing touch with the five senses of them. Art elaborates what isn't there and elaborates what could be there; this is the way art toys with what a society has already recognized consensually as basically "real."

Micah Lexier [b. Canada 1960, lives in New York]
A Minute of My Time: July 17, 2000: in situ view 2005
Laser jet-cut steel, posts, 122 x 214 cm
Photograph: Robert Birch
Courtesy of the artist and Birch Libralato Gallery, Toronto

> When theories ... do not afford intellectual assistance in
> framing ideas and beliefs about values adequate to direct
> action, the gap must be filled by other means. If intelligent
> method is lacking, prejudice, the pressure of immediate
> circumstance, self-interest and class interest, traditional
> customs, institutions of accidental historic origin, are not
> lacking, and they tend to take the place of intelligence.[25]

As much as I respect methodical intelligence, I am going to
continue parading my cogitations about imagination without
offering any method for distinguishing between "imaginative"
and "unimaginative." As much as we need intellectual
assistance to frame ideas and beliefs, I am marshalling
extreme caution to avoid judgments that grade imagination
as if it could transpire in bad, worse, worst or good, better and
best forms. This seems urgent. It seems imperative to me to
prevent arousal, according to such gradations, of a sneer at
someone(s) else. I am wary of people in enclaves of extreme
monetary wealth staking a claim on everything of value while
designating the citizens of less financially endowed enclaves to

25 *Dewey, p 265*

be inferior custodians of pricey objects and valuable ideas. The differences between life in enclaves of extreme monetary wealth and our enclaves of material luxury, not to mention enclaves of desperation, are too great already without someone exploiting so-called gradations of imaginative quality in order to justify their own greed.

As I reflect upon the experience of imagining, there is a way of speaking about it that is unfamiliar in everyday speech but necessary for me. This is to emphasize, as I have mentioned, that imagination is a valuable illusion. To speak of imagination as illusory, rather than as a mental process that creates illusions, may seem odd, but to do so introduces the theoretical bias of these reflections on luxury and ethics. This bias is complex and unfamiliar perhaps, which may make it too topsy-turvy to seem credible. This bias, however, makes my response to Dewey possible. Dewey, pining for intellectual assistance, would have received my conjecture of ethical imagining as nothing if not intellectual. And my bias ("to speak of imagination as illusory experience") uncovers aspects of imagining that citizens of an enclave of luxury can well afford.

I am thinking of imagining not only as a phenomenon, but also as an experience. It is so easy to say in English "She's got imagination," as if imagination were a pocketful of loose change. If I were to state, "The gospel singers and the congregation are making Jesus," would I be making sense? What I would mean is that the devout congregation is sustaining its belief with a joyous communal practice. They are creating as well as experiencing "consensus as to what is loved."[26] In this way I underscore imagining as a way of participating in one's culture. I underscore imagination as socially sustained; "*practice* gives the words ['Jesus' or 'imagining'] their sense."[27] Imagining is not as transient as common sense might claim, nor incongruous with everyday living.

26 "*Rerum quas diligit concordi communione*," *Augustine*, De Civilitate Dei contra Paganos, *Book 19:24*

27 *Italics in the original, Ludwig Wittgenstein*, Culture and Value, *ed. G.H. von Wright, trans. Peter Winch (Chicago: University of Chicago Press, 1980), p 85 ["Die Praxis gibt den Worten ihren Sinn."]*

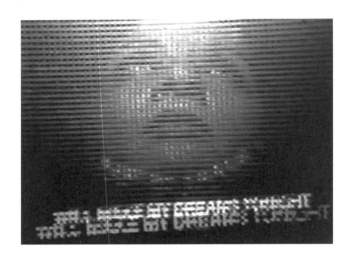

Mark Gane [b. Canada 1953] and Martha Johnson [b. Canada 1950]
Still from ONLY YOU 1987
Muffin Music promotional video
Courtesy of Muffin Music

Imagination is a name given to something that is not a thing. I spurn quantification and precision when I speak of imagining. I won't get specific in logical terms. Instead I speak of imagining as an illusory experience, initiated communally (even if at first the community is someone[s] willing to nurture their infant). This interpretation of imagining (and, in what follows, of reason and of ethics and other intangibles in communal life) is inspired by the theoretical writings of the late object relations psychoanalyst D.W. Winnicott (1896-1971).[28] Object relations psychoanalytic theory calls attention to communal experiences that do not necessarily aim at material outcomes. These communal, non-material aspects of interpersonal and social experiences are the "working fictions" communities sustain. In this sense, what philosophers might include in the term "values," a psychoanalyst would have included in the term "illusions." (Scientists, for example, work together all the time for the sake of illusions that they term "hypotheses.") Illusions are experiences, to use Sartre's words, emerging from "... syntheses of external elements and psychical elements."[29] Obviously this understanding of illusion is not what is meant in ordinary speech.

28 *See* Playing and Reality.
29 *Jean-Paul Sartre*, The Psychology of Imagination, *trans. Bernard Frechtman (N.Y. Washington Square Press, 1966) p 25*

Object relations theory matured within an intellectual discourse that by the end of the twentieth century was not disputed: binary thinking is inadequate for careful contemplation. In psychoanalytic thinking, by the time World War II ended, it was necessary to identify the clinical harm of dualistic thinking. It was urgent to articulate that an illusory experience (the experience of imagining) would not be judged or censored on the basis of probability and measurable dimensions; deception, fake, fantasy would not *a priori* be synonyms for illusory experience. What I am saying, although the object relations psychoanalysts did not, is that these terms, like true and false, genuine and fake, fantasy and reality, etc. are best suited for the extremes of human experience.

These terms claim validity for simplistic opposites. In contrast, according to object relations psychoanalytic theory, ordinary people sustain illusions in between such extremes, which is to say that pure precision with dualistic terms is not crucial in everyday life. It is more probable that situations are immeasurable, ambiguous, indeed messy. And this is to say that to demand precise dualistic language for everyday situations impedes rather than clarifies ordinary appraisements. No one waits for "the fake bus" to go away because they want "the genuine bus;" we get it that "Coke is the real thing [and any other cola is the phony thing]" even though "Coca-Cola is Coca-Cola and Pepsi-Cola is not Coca-Cola" is useless as a mere fact. In 2002 many people believed in the brute perception of "an Axis of Evil." "An Alliance of Good" is simplistic beyond credibility. All this is hardly worth spelling out, except to accentuate that grammar may authorize what ordinary life invalidates and vice versa.

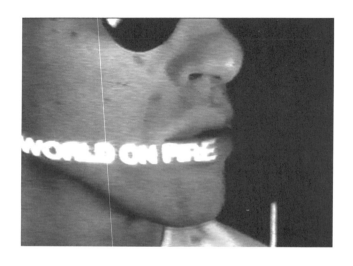

Mark Gane and Martha Johnson
Still from ONLY YOU 1987
Muffin Music promotional video
Courtesy of Muffin Music

In the course of generating a method of analysis that is not dominated by dualistic thinking, an object relations psycho-analysis of everyday life is based on the possibility of recognizing and respecting all that transpires between fantasy (the as-yet-unprecedented means by which manufacturers might monitor consumers) and reality (a flesh and blood man loping along in baggy track pants), or between good and evil, between sane and insane, between being and nothingness, between yes and no, etc.

There must be a way of reminding ourselves (and representing to ourselves) that we can afford to perceive the full range of human experience that is intermediate. At this point in history in enclaves of luxury it costs less than one iota to acknowledge the expansive range of experience that cannot be taken literally. And would it cost a psyche enormously to appreciate *that this expansive range of experience is also our privilege?* Surely the psychoanalyst Karen Horney (1885–1952) was not one hundred per cent accurate when she claimed that

> It may be said that we are opposed to nothing so much as to the realization that we must change some attitude of our own.[30]

30 *Karen Horney MD*, The Neurotic Personality of Our Time *(New York: W.W. Norton, 1937) p 47*

Dr. Horney would have predicted that people living in enclaves of luxury refuse to perceive "an expansive range of experience that cannot be taken literally," because this attitude change would precipitate anxiety and self-doubt. Dr. Horney would have predicted that people living in enclaves of luxury would not acknowledge the pervasive relevance of imagination because the emotional cost of changing the relevant attitude is too high. Better not to acknowledge the privilege of imagining, lest we begin to admit to all the other privileges as well.

Just how taxing would it be to acknowledge how everyday ambiguities elude dualistic terms? How pricey is "an attitude change" that would prevent taking everything literally? Is "an attitude change" too expensive? To speak of ideas as if they are things, is this one of the great bargains to be had in an enclave of luxury? Even in an enclave of luxury, is the reification of ideas somehow a necessity?

In enclaves of luxury would toying with the term "illusory experience" require any more investment of mental effort than toying with the idea of "designer genes"? All this is another way of proposing that illusory experiences are not rare; it's the concept of "illusory experience" that is rare. Surely we move quite naturally in a sea of impressions. Surely we are already accustomed to "participation in a reality, in a plenitude"[31] of intermediate experience, but don't quite get around to finding the words for it.

I can no longer take illusory experiences for granted. They are of great value because they are lived through; we live through them. These illusory experiences are lived through as infinite organic elaborations upon abstract terms (With very few hideous exceptions—and with very few wondrous exceptions—terms such as pure vs. impure, right vs. wrong, certain vs. uncertain, saintly vs. sinful, etc. are abstract descriptives). These illusory experiences can be lived through as countless elaborations upon the organic world.

The term "illusory experience" will be my fulcrum for raising imagination into an ethical atmosphere.

31 *Marcel, p 99 [quoting from Marcel's* De Refus a L'invocation, *p 123]*

Among all possible worthy intangibles invented and socially sustained, this essay is offered as benefactor to imagination.

So far, in enclaves of material luxury, children are often born into groups that offer the experience of imagination. There is nothing odd about being born into a group that enjoys the way imagination transforms objects and situations. The value of imagination is bestowed. By now, in the twenty-first century of Western Christian influence, the word *imagination* can be taken for granted as well established in the English language.

In the psychoanalytic sense, the idea that imagination is real and valuable constitutes an illusion, an illusion that requires maintenance as a real experience. Imagination, made real and valuable, is an illusion sustained in conversation. Every once in a while in a community someone will talk to someone(s) else about imagination and imagining. Imagination is still practiced, although it seems prized in children and downplayed in adults.

James Lahey [b. Canada 1961]
Site view of elevator at Le Germain Hotel, Toronto 2003
James Lahey (photography) and Hélèn Dorion (writing)
Photograph: Michael Cullen
Courtesy of the artist

Advertisers know the power that imagining connotes. Corny ads depict the so-called dreams that corporations make come so-called true. In ads, imagining, like so many cultural practices, serves to aggrandize a product; this is the craft of advertising. It is just that when I see these advertisements, I see how imagination is trivialized. When it is hilariously trivialized I laugh along with everyone else. It can get paradoxical however: unimaginative bosses have stifled the imagination of the artisans making advertisements such that the advertisements trivialize imagination. Meanwhile the trivialization of imagination goes unnoticed by the audience. For the audience, is it that imagination will always flourish so why worry, or that imagination is not worth that much anyway so why bother fighting for it? Or is it that imagination is something that happens to other people, sort of like a rare brain infection? Maybe the chances are one in a zillion that imagination will be the foremost experience of your life, and then you die. Meanwhile, what is "really" good to *have*? Or have not?

We call that which is in itself worthy of pursuit more final than that which is worthy of pursuit for the sake of something else, and that which is never desirable for the sake of something else more final than the things that are desirable both in themselves and for the sake of that other thing, and therefore we call final without qualification that which is always desirable in itself and never for the sake of something else.[32]

By Aristotle's criteria of "final good," imagining, conversation and ethics are worthy of pursuit, and possibly among those pursuits that are "final without qualification," maybe not. I am dreaming that there is still plenty of time and opportunity in enclaves of luxury to reconsider much without proclaiming what is "final."

32 Ethica Nicomachea, *(Chicago: Great Books Foundation, n.d.) p 9*

There may even be groups of people who bestow upon imagining an intrinsic goodness according to Aristotle's criteria for "good." What Aristotle reasoned as good, is itself an illusion that could be evoked, sustained and propagated by a willing group of people. To sustain Aristotle's hypothesis of good, a group of people would insist upon the possibility that there is such a quality as "good." It is not unimaginable that such a group of people could understand that whatever is good, even according to Aristotle, is elusive, contingent, complex, debatable, yet still exceedingly precious.

The value—also the vulnerability—of any idea resides in this necessity of public and personal sustenance in consciousness and in conversation.

Iain Baxter&
Reflected San Francisco Beauty Spots (Buddha in Golden Gate Park) 1979
From a suite of photoetchings with colour aquatint, printed in black and
pink at Crown Point Press. Edition of 20, 89 x 76 cm
Courtesy of the artist

Shaun Gladwell [b. Australia 1972]
Pataphysical Man, 2005 production still
DVD, 13:00 minutes, 16:9, silent
Performance: Daniel Esteve Pomares, videography: Gotaro Uematsu
Courtesy the artist and Sherman Galleries, Sydney

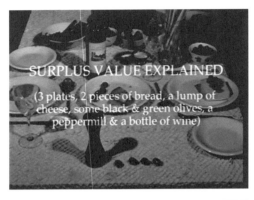

Richard Grayson [b. England 1958]
2 stills from *Various Things Explained*, 1998, *2. Marx's theory of surplus value*
Video, 20 mins
Courtesy of the artist

Everything that I have mentioned so far is a prelude to the idea of "ethical imagining," with a reminder that reasoning, imagining, apprehending what is good, as well as consuming, are experiences, not things, and flimsier still, something(s) conjured by groups of people. These experiences gain meaning as culture to the extent we understand that "culture is an observance."[33] Perhaps an utter stranger could study North American society as an object. To us within North America our cultures are our practices, not merely the things we have.

As I continue these reflections elaborating upon the idea of ethical imagining, it seems important at first to consider ethical imagining as a perturbing lens; ethical imagining would elaborate what isn't there and would elaborate what could be there, as any imaginative act does. Yet I deliberately glom "perturbing" onto "ethical." Here in my enclave of luxury, of all the thousands of adjectives in the English language, I am going to offer "perturbing" and "ethical" as sisters.

33 *Wittgenstein*, Culture and Value, *1980, p 83*

In keeping with object relations psychoanalytic theory, I will be contemplating ethical imagining with its particular, perhaps peculiar understanding as illusion. Illusions come into being consensually along a spectrum of experiences, at one extreme of which the term delusion would apply (We know that delusions also may come into being consensually. I seem to recall Nietzsche having written how "Insanity in humans is rare. In nations it is the rule." Perhaps it is the same with delusions). At the other end of this spectrum there would be what is termed reality. And yet so-called reality is a concept whose criteria are debatable. By whatever means it is consensually upheld, reality is not a once-and-for-all verifiable fact.

Reality is inexhaustible and there must be infinite ways in which it can be thought.[34]

An illusion, in this psychoanalytic sense, is the experience of an idea made real by being practiced in a social milieu. In a social milieu people contribute their personal knowledge, memories, longings—and their choice to sustain the illusion. Some of our most precious illusions (reason, imagination, reality, money) seem vaguely understandable through day-to-day behaviour and have a long history in Western parlance. The illusory experiences of imagination and reason are vitally connected with finding a way of life and ways of speaking about our way of life. In enclaves of luxury people have made these ideas in effect real, which doesn't insure whatsoever that the experience of them can be taken for granted.

34 *Stuart Hampshire, intro.* Benedict de Spinoza: Ethics *(Toronto: Penguin, 1996) p ix*

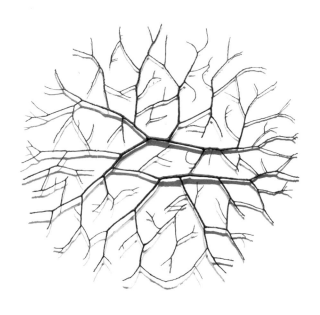

Hossein Valamanesh [b. Iran 1949, Lives in Australia]
Fallen branch, 2005
Bronze, 60 cm diameter x 7 cm
Photograph: Paul Green
Courtesy of the artist and Greenaway Art Gallery, Adelaide

I acknowledge that I am offering my hypotheses like a glass of greenish water in which I tell you there are amoebae. I depend on you to care what an amoeba is, its shape always changing, a transparent entity one recognizes best when it is moving, or by the granules it ingests. I depend on you to be curious, even thrilled by the idea of amoebae. And if you are living in an enclave of luxury, it is likely you have already learned how to recognize an amoeba.

In the consciousness of people—and in the choices these people make—if it is possible to conceive of illusion-making as good, as imagining and reasoning might be, maybe there is an illusion of ethical imagining to be conjured. In their social interplay groups could conjure and nourish the experience of ethical imagining.

I am going on and on about imagination. In enclaves of luxury like the one where I live the illusion of imagination is sustained because it is appreciated; its appreciation is taught. I am assuming you, as was I, were taught what imagination is at the time you were busy imagining, and therefore we notice that acts of imagination are committed every day. Maybe every day there are also circumstances to which ethical imagining could contribute.

My purposes require ethical imagining that is vaguely human, not an objectively perceived phenomenon.

What if ordinary, unselfconscious means for sustaining these illusions are insufficient to protect them? Is it possible to perceive the vulnerability of these illusions? Isn't it important to acknowledge that taking these illusions for granted is a privilege?

Within these questions another question is nestled: what if there are influences in enclaves of luxury—as we often assume there are in enclaves of desperation—that turn ethical imagining into foolishness? What if this is the test (and the task) of a body politic honest enough to acknowledge luxury as its

Tanya Rusnak [b. Canada 1968]
The Grey Film of Dust (burning mountain, Rr V1) 2004
Gouache drawing on vellum, 37 x 37 cm
Courtesy of the artist and Trépanier Baer Gallery, Calgary

Wyn Gelynse [b. Netherlands 1947, lives in Canada]
Theory/Practice Ball or Practice/Theory Ball, 2005-06
Sand-engraved onto a 7 cm diameter glass ball, edition of 20
Courtesy of the artist

fundament: whether something precious is abundant of course; and whether something of value (such as ethical imagining) is endangered because we are materially over-rewarded.

Shall we assume ethical imagination is always present among all possible imaginations (literary, criminal, lyrical, culinary, diabolical, medical, philosophical, religious, creative, maternal, destructive, legal, sexual, architectural, exploitative, veterinary, technological, and on and on)? And if always present some-where, is ethical imagination always contributing somehow?

How would ethical imagination be depicted?

If it is not depicted, how could it be acknowledged as valuable?

If it is so unnoticeable it isn't recognizable enough to be considered valuable, how could it be sustained communally as an illusory experience?

Without the illusory experience of ethical imagining, do we already have more than enough interpretations of ethical? Is there no longer any point to going on and on about ethics? Is the evolution of ethics—or what we have imagined to be ethics—complete? Or could it be that the illusory experience (the memory) of ethical is out-of-date and irrelevant?

What if a group of people realized that we can

> ... share a respect for the illusion of ethical imagining,
> and we wish to form a group on the basis of the
> similarity of our illusory experience of it.

With gratitude to Wittgenstein[35], certainly for the sake of my
hypothesis of a cultural practice I name as "ethical imagining,"
I have pondered what relationships a group of fortunate
people would enjoy with each other if they believed in ethical
imagining. Reading object relations psychoanalytic theory
(and reading between the lines of it as well) the next phase
of my method for conjuring "ethical imagining" will be to
suggest prototypical values that might guide a group of
people in their observance of [practicing] "ethical imagining."

35 *Wittgenstein, p 74, "Nothing is more important for teaching us to understand
the concepts that we have than creating fictitious ones."*

Arthur Schopenhauer noted that "teachers of ethics are really in agreement: *Neminem laede, imo omnes, quantum potes juva,*" which is to say "Injure no one; on the contrary, help everyone as much as you can."[36] Spinoza also described an ethical relationship as one in which the effect would be "to make one another confidant that they will do nothing which could harm others [*se invicem securos reddant, se nihil acturos, quod possit in alterius adnum cedere*]."[37]

As a psychoanalyst I am duty bound to refrain altogether from advising individuals in my hypothetical group to obey Schopenhauer's or Spinoza's (or any) truisms. As a psychoanalytic researcher, I could try to discover conditions (circumstantial, intermediate, and intrapsychic) that favour adherence to these truisms. As a fellow member of the group, knowing what I know psychoanalytically, the best I could hope for

36 On the Basis of Morality, *trans. E.F.J. Payne (Providence and Oxford: Berghahn Books, 1995) p 69*
37 *Spinoza,* Ethics, *Book IV, proposition xiv, corollary 2, Scholium*

Caitlin Reid [b. Scotland 1966, lives in Australia]
Torso, 1999
Candle soot on Dutch etching paper, 112 x 92 cm
Courtesy of the artist

would be this: my fellow group members desire with all their hearts to practice illusory experiences of these truisms. As a fellow member of the group I would hope that among us our respect for these truisms is similar enough to be one of the entice-ments for our conviviality. If so, these truisms would become, as it were, "our observance." We would make a practice of these truisms such that they would readily make sense to anyone.

All this is to delineate that we would enter situations together trusting each other *primum non nocere*,[38] as if somehow playing around with this unambiguous Hippocratic advice and ethical imagining were inextricable.

38 *from The Hippocratic Oath, "... First of all to do no harm..."*

The natural thing is playing, and the highly sophisticated twentieth century phenomenon is psychoanalysis. It must be of value to the analyst to be constantly reminded not only of what is owed to Freud but also of what we owe to the natural and universal thing called playing.[39]

Object relations psychoanalysts assume that the propensity to play is as innate in humans as it is in kittens. That's fine, but if I take the trouble to derive ethical imagining from play, whether this bestows upon the supposedly ethical a "normal" or "natural" origin makes no difference to me.

Although it no longer makes a difference to me whether there is a psychoanalysis of ethical imagining, it is possible to devise one, summarized for the next six paragraphs, available for those readers who are curious about the psychoanalytic bias of this essay.

39 *Winnicott, p 48*

Object relations psychoanalysis has made salient, evocative claims for play. The centrality of play evolving within a nurturing environment and its fruition into adult productivity is explicit.

> This intermediate area of experience, unchallenged in respect to its belonging to inner or external (shared) reality, constitutes the greater part of the infant's experience, and throughout life is retained in the intense experiencing that belongs to the arts and to religion and to imaginative living, and to creative scientific work.[40]

I contend that it is possible for a group of people to recognize an intermediate area of experience when it is happening: embellishing a favourite story at a dinner party, toying with possibilities for re-arranging the furniture, joking with one's spouse about Paris Hilton, conversing with your dog, all ordinary stuff, and yet the brew of subjectivity and objects, of intangibles and the embodied world is wondrous. Such are the sustainable illusions of reliably safe situations, however transient, during which there is no life and death struggle for survival of body, or sense of self, or of dignity.

40 *Winnicott, p 65*

Don Jean-Louis [b. Canada 1937]
...*to sleep awake* c. 1974
Photograph, dimensions variable
Courtesy of the artist

Ludocentric psychoanalysis proposes that caring for and caring about one's children are impossible without playfulness. Good-enough nurturers are generous and relaxed when they offer safe experiences (of objects and sounds) to the baby for baby to receive, distort and return—as embodying (e.g. acting out) their connectedness. Object relations theory regards all the forms of infant communication, including facial expressions, gestures, mimicry, actions, and complex playing as infants interpreting their reality. Supposedly, playing creates a discovery of familiar and unfamiliar, and an experience of what occurs crawling, toddling, slipping and thinking between familiar and unfamiliar. Play is the child's ongoing representation of their existence. (This contrasts enormously with Freud's hypothesis of toy/symbol as a substitute for an unattainable object of desire.)

Object relations theory reads playing into adult cultural practices. As well as when adults are delighting in avocational pursuits or hobbies, playing encompasses the initiation of scientific hypotheses or invention of methods to test these. Many find aspects of their employment conducive to playfulness. And one may play with children. Playing continues into adult-hood, evolving and variegating formally and informally. All this is obvious: David Beckham playing soccer as a profession; a vice president playing squash against the assistant vice president; a group of neighbours playing softball every weekend; two uncles playing checkers at every family reunion;

four administrative assistants looking at fabric swatches daydreaming they might redecorate the office; a couple fielding names for children who aren't even conceived yet; old friends ad libbing quips at a dinner party; and of course, a psychoanalyst with her analysand; a composer at her piano; a philosopher toying with a neologism; an architect doodling while talking on the telephone—and so on.

This list illustrates a gradual transition from professional sport to unselfconscious doodling. At one end of this spectrum is technically demanding play, in which mastery includes stunning instants of physical innovation. At the other end a highly trained and technically expert professional is scribbling absent-mindedly without commitment to the results.

In his depiction of the psychoanalytic setting, Freud unwittingly characterized a playful milieu as it would later be understood by object relations theory:

> ... an intermediate region... [It is] a piece of real experience but one that has been made possible by especially favourable conditions, and is of a provisional nature.[41]

41 Remembering, Repeating and Working-Through (Further Recommendations on the Technique of Psycho-analysis II) [*Standard Edition, 1914*] *pp 147 and 150*

Freud's observation and the above list, however, imply there is a difference between playing and not playing. These descriptions are, in a sense, too objective. Most people have met someone whose interpretation of life is as rough as rugby and necessitates a referee. And there are people whose interpretation of life is as calculating as a game of chess. There are those for whom life is one hopscotch after another. To mention this is to enlist analogy, but I want to evoke the heart of playing, an attitude that includes a willingness for improvisation and unscripted mucking about, with a potential for surprise and the laughter that surprise can kindle.

Playfulness refers to spontaneity, novelty, indeterminacy, and yet a special attentiveness. Playfulness is a certain attitude toward opportunities; a generous attitude toward an object or moment discovered. In what can seem like a complete suspension of expectations and progress, playful psyche and opportunity become aspects of the same creation. I am accenting playfulness in which we are

> ... maintaining ourselves actively in a permeable state, and there is a mysterious interchange between this free act and the gift granted in response to it.[42]

42 *Marcel, p 38*

The so-called ethical conditions sketched up to now are reliant upon a debatable assumption: that there can be trust between people, though not necessarily in everything every time. I am (again) beginning with a question "If trust is possible, then what?" If trust is possible, could two or more people trust each other *primum non nocere*? I chose this phrase to begin sketching an ethical social nexus because of my emphasis on people trusting one another from the outset not to do harm. They could trust one another to begin the interaction wary of whether they might hurt one another. This is not to say that I am advocating people agree ahead of time they will do anything to avoid causing distress or pain (I am rather hoping this essay itself may cause a little worthwhile pain). Rather, I would say I am picturing some people fully trusting each other to have first and foremost an aversion to causing pain to other people. The emphasis is upon a capacity for trust, not on a probability no one will feel hurt. I do wonder whether such relationships would happen by default. It seems far-fetched to expect them to happen by decree. But an ethical social nexus begins to form when some citizens have a capacity for trust.

Added to this trust of each other's commitment *primum non nocere* is the assumption that everyone in the group will value conversation. Then added to these suppositions is the possibility that these several people actually abhor objectifying other human beings or perceiving them as means in the service of an agenda.

These suppositions rely on you, the thinking reader, to provisionally suspend skepticism about the probability such people exist, and suspend your own demand that if such people exist, their abhorrence of objectification be accounted for.

Perhaps it would be less idealistic to imagine that within this hypothetical group, each abhors objectifying others — without being in a position anyway to objectify in grand style. For instance, a shopkeeper who knows she must sell so many pounds of vegetables or fruit each day to meet her overhead expenses may, just before closing time on a stormy evening, feel relief and anticipation that if the three customers in her shop at that moment buy produce enough to total $24, she will have accumulated all her overhead expenses for the next two days. As she holds out her weary hand for the final six

Vikky Alexander [b. Canada, 1959]
Untitled Chair 2003
Mirrored glass, edition of 3, 93 x 40.5 x 40.5 cm
Courtesy of the artist and Trépanier Baer Gallery, Calgary

dollars, she may barely notice the customer. This customer is emaciated, possibly starving. The shopkeeper is too fatigued to look at her intently. Instead the shopkeeper is looking at the four loonies, seven quarters, four nickels and five pennies in that scrawny hand. Expertly, the shopkeeper confirms the tally. During this transaction, the shopkeeper will have objectified the woman, reduced her to mere economic function. Suppose, however, that the shopkeeper has experienced ethical imagining before. As soon as she lies down in bed that night, her eyes closed, she recalls the customer in more detail; she realizes the woman to have been in a very frail state. And then what would the shopkeeper's so-called ethical imagining look like?

Suppose there was a business directed and managed by people who all share the prevalent illusory experience of free will. One of their policies is to hire for certain promotional functions only women who are six feet tall with a weight of 120 pounds. This amounts to requiring that only people in a state of starvation could get and keep the job. These directors and managers hear of, perhaps watch their employees swallowing toilet paper dunked in black coffee, retching up bits of lettuce and injecting cocaine on the inside of their thighs. If they imagine an employee's desiccated liver and ovaries, oozy red esophagus and unravelling gray matter, what has this got to do with so-called ethical imagining? Whether or not such scenarios seem likely or unlikely, I continue the make-believe of a group of basically imaginative people, a group formed on the basis of shared illusion of the experience of ethical imagining (or, if this is really a new idea, a group formed on the basis of the hypothesis that there is such a practice as ethical imagining). I understand that all I accomplish may be to dramatize my psychoanalytic bias.

Given the impetus *primum non nocere*, it would not be contradictory to suppose that in our enclave of luxury:

We would converse gladly;

We would delight in curiosity;

Certainly we would abhor objectification of any person anywhere; this would include abhorrence of reacting to another person as a mere function of our own agenda;

Each of us would maintain equanimity about holding individual or group power;

We would never enforce judgments on the basis of delusional language (inside vs. outside; sense vs. nonsense; real vs. fantasy; possible vs. impossible, etc.);

It would be our joy, whenever possible, to remove obstacles to playfulness;

If we witnessed someone(s) who rarely had the opportunity to participate in situations like ours, our saddened response would include reconsideration of the relevance of their situation to our enclave of luxury;

After many conversations we might even come to believe that the illusory experience we had conjured—ethical imagining —keeps us together even while we are dispersed across North America working in separate enclaves of luxury.

The above relationships and values are not directly attributable to a particular philosopher. Instead, these are my educated guesses; I believe these are some of the consequences of congregating (virtually if not literally) on the basis of shared respect for the illusory experience of ethical imagining. The philosophical background obviously includes Schopenhauer's and Spinoza's truisms. And it includes the philosophical milieu out of which object relations psychoanalysis emerged. For now the list above is in the foreground, a string of hypotheses.

Atelier Bow-Wow [Japan]
Kiosk for vegetables (interior detail) 1992
Courtesy of Atelier Bow-Wow

Added to this trust of each other's commitment *primum non nocere* is an assumption that the people in this group will converse with each other. Curiosity is implicated in this concatenation of so-called ethical imagining because it seems to me that whenever a psyche supposes or wonders "What if? ...How?" reasoning and imagining ensue. Curiosity seems loosely tethered to playing. The fortunate people in their enclave are said to avoid interrupting anyone who was playing. This feature of a purported ethical social nexus obviously has the imprimatur of object relations psychoanalytic theory. This theory emphasizes a social environment for spontaneous play (as well as, in addition to, the obvious pleasure of official games).

Make believe that the individuals who join this group are people who value camaraderie and believe that creativity could include generating ethical circumstances. These people will want to articulate their living conditions (explicitly and/or implicitly), and some of them may be able to represent the living conditions artfully; there will be reciprocity between their circumstances and their imaginations. How could ethical imagining not ripen? How could a group of people conscious of what is at stake in ethical imagining immediately prefer to give priority to materialism instead? To realize an ethos of materialism is insuffient (as well as, in a sense, emotionally grueling) would clear a time and space for ethical imagining. How could something so prominent in a group's consciousness go undepicted? (Although so far it has not been depicted yet in this essay.)

Maybe it is hard to believe that such a group would form, but we know that if such a group were artists, their work would reflect their situation. Hard to believe as it may be, their situation could likewise affirm the ethical imagining in their work. There is, as well, the possibility that any such group would strive to represent their situation somehow in a literary and plastic form, using a basic or a sophisticated technique (or, most likely, a technique somewhere between basic and sophisticated).

Paradoxically, in describing this luxurious enclave of people gathered on the basis of a shared illusion, I have listed their relationships and values as if I already know what an ethical milieu is. Probably Schopenhauer would not have pronounced this milieu to be idiosyncratic or arbitrary. Maybe Spinoza wouldn't have either. As I said, I didn't imagine this so-called ethical milieu *de novo*. I read it between the lines: I have read and re-read my favourite psychoanalytic writings for so many years that I have begun to reinterpret them as more than clinical observations and theories. In addition to what object relations psychoanalysis conveyed about "health" (respect for the illusory experience of which physicians, nurses, patients etc. have formed groups) I have read ethics into it as well. Activist psychoanalytic scholars had been doing this throughout the twentieth century.

Atelier Bow-Wow [Japan]
Kiosk for vegetables 1992
Courtesy of Atelier Bow-Wow

It would be our joy, whenever possible, to remove obstacles to playfulness.

A scene is easier to visualize when described as an external environment. A so-called ethical scene may call for descriptions of what people do and say. And patterns of saying and doing activate patterns of thinking, and, of course vice versa (or writing an essay would be futile). In psychoanalytic theory it is axiomatic that familiar settings are internalized. An external environment is a matrix for perception, expectations and interpretations that constitute "making sense." This is to say that interacting with one's setting induces a kind of mental (and probably neurophysiologic) mapping; external factors supposedly have their counterparts in attitude or mental ambiance.

Playfulness, I propose, is the setting for ethical imagining, and playing is prominent in enclaves of luxury.

One could interpret playfulness as a social intangible. And here is the connection I am making with ethical imagining: playfulness often occurs in situations that have much in common with a safe-enough social nexus, such as trust, reliability, suspension of penalties enforced by dualistic delusions (such as real or fantasy, and, paradoxically, dualistic delusions such as evil or good, correct or incorrect. I will certainly return later to the paradox of including evil vs. good as delusional even in ethical imagining).

Of every individual who has reached to the stage of being a unit with a limiting membrane and an outside and an inside, it can be said that there is an inner reality to that individual, an inner world that can be rich or poor and can be at peace or in a state of war. This helps, but is it enough? My claim is that if there is a need for this double statement, there is also need for a triple one: the third part of the life of a human being, a part that we cannot ignore, is an intermediate area of experiencing, to which inner reality and external life both contribute...[43]

The ethical significance of this interpretation of human development is that although one has acknowledged the binary language of "inner and outer" (Freud's Reality Principle) or "objective and subjective" (The Technological Ethos) it is still possible to conceive of an "intermediate area" between these polarities. According to object relations theory so-called culture (contrasted provisionally for the sake of clarity to technologies of survival) is an elaboration of this intermediate area. These elaborations include infusing what one perceives with deliberate subjectivity, suspending the compulsion to

43 *Winnicott, pp 2-3*

impose categories while granting ambiguity and relishing paradox. These elaborations have been called poetic revisions but not in the sense of formal literary technique. Playfulness recovers ideas, perceptions and interpretations from strict dualism (which I have slandered as both abstract and delusional). Dualistic language has expressivity—but its clarity can be misleading. To depend as masterfully on dualistic language as Freud did, would be in a sense delusional, a denial of the plenitude of day-to-day experience that is engaging, inconclusive and unselfconscious.

An everyday life that is engaging, inconclusive and unself-conscious does not interfere with Spinoza's truism of existing and working without intentional injury to oneself or other. It is congenial to Galbraith's observation of North American affluence where citizens spend their life in clean and physically comfortable surroundings with some opportunity for applying their thought to the day's work. In an enclave of luxury one would not expect playfulness to put all this at risk.

According to object relations theory, playing is the prototype of creativity and creativity is allied with sociability. (Freud imagined creativity as an aspect of narcissism.) Whether rooted in narcissism or sociability, Freud would have considered an invocation of ethical imagining to be futile:

> In my experience I have found little that is good about human beings on the whole. In my experience most of them are trash no matter whether they publicly subscribe to this or that ethical doctrine or none at all.[44]

> The element of truth...which people are so ready to disavow, is that men are not gentle creatures who want to be loved, and who at the most can defend themselves if they are attacked; they are, on the contrary, creatures among whose instinctual endowments is to be reckoned a powerful share of aggressiveness. As a result, their neighbour is for them not only a potential helper or

44 Psycho-analysis and faith; the letters of Sigmund Freud and Oskar Pfister. *[1907-1926] eds. Heinrich Meng and Ernst L. Freud; trans. Eric Mosbacher (London: Hogarth Press, 1963)*

sexual object, but also someone who tempts them to
satisfy their aggressiveness on him, to exploit his capacity
for work without compensation, to use him sexually
without his consent, to seize his possessions, to humiliate
him, to cause him pain, to torture and to kill him. *Homo
homini lupus*. ["Man is a wolf to Man."][45]

This is not a credible description of baby care.

Whether or not play is from the moment of birth inextricable
from psychological and social development, I am proclaiming
the reality of baby care as analogous enough to an ethical
relationship (Though it is not a version of paradise or utopia,
and it's no *Republic*, no *City of the Sun*, and not an endpoint,
like Augustine's *City of God*). Even if superficially "baby care"
seems a commonplace, even, in fact because it is a commonplace, it could be an ethical template. As a template it approximates
a social nexus (in an enclave of luxury) where (along with the

45 *Freud*, Civilization and Its Discontents *[1939] trans. A.A. Brill
    (NY: W. W. Norton and Sons, 1962) p 58, in* Ethics, Book IV,
    *Proposition XXXVIII, Scholium; in contrast, Spinoza repeated what he
    heard as a richly ambivalent yet nevertheless "common saying" in his day,
    hominem homini Deum esse, e.g. "Man is a God to Man."*

task of survival) the intangibles generated are worth considering. Not just object relations theory, but also parents themselves would hardly find baby care devoid of ethical implications. As a template, it is vaguely good enough and relevant enough for now. As for ethical imagining, it cannot be substantiated by proven facts. All I can do is fool around with a notion of ethical imagining. Like baby care, ethical imagining might be possible without so-called hard science. And it wouldn't require genius either.

If my ideas are true and universal then each reader will have personal illustrations. [46]

For one writes only half the book...the other half is with the reader.[47]

46 *Winnicott, p 89*

47 *Joseph Conrad quoted in ed.'s intro. from a letter,* Heart of Darkness, *ed. D.C.R&A. Goonetilleke (Peterborough ON: Broadview Press, 1999) p 144*

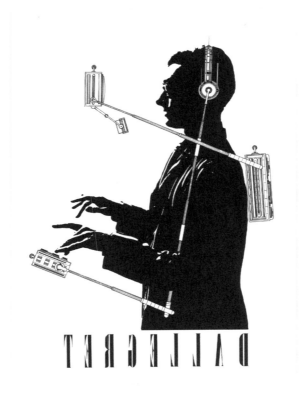

François Dallegret
IntroConversoMatic, 1964
Photomontage and China ink drawing
© François Dallegret/SODRAC (2007)

Anything your reader can do for himself leave it to him.[48]

The scientific method requires that the experiment do all the work. This is the case with logical and mathematical proofs also. The audience who receives the results of the scientific method is not obligated to fill in what has not yet been proven. Whatever I am writing here, I am not following the scientific method. I believe that what readers can do for themselves is bountiful, and I welcome gladly more than half.

Nothing about ethics has been proven. Ethics then might be a way of talking about an aspect of human relatedness where proof can't be expected. Ethics, like poetry, is in between what is certain (recognition of the words in which it is written) and what is contributed by the reader's knowledge, memories, longings, and interpretations. The reader is also going to contribute skepticism and refutation of course. Ethical imaginings rely, just as poetry does, on the readers' experience and, it is crucial to repeat, experience in an enclave of luxury, where material goods may obscure non-material bounty.

48   *Wittgenstein, p 77*

Mikala Dwyer [b. Australia 1959]
From the installation *Free Speech* 2005
Modeling clay, wood, blackboard paint, chalk, glitter and table
Dimensions variable
Courtesy of the artist and Darren Knight Gallery, Sydney

I am filching a model for an ethical social nexus from object relations psychoanalytic theory. Psychoanalysts were way later than parents to comprehend that the child must not merely survive, but also thrive. Baby tending is all around us. Acts of tenderness may be sensual and personal, but they are not odd or even original. Baby care is devotional. As a model it need only be vaguely good enough. Even if it is barely good enough I will take heart in Wittgenstein's saying that

> Nothing is more important for teaching us to understand the concepts that we have than creating fictitious ones. [49]

I am offering the fictitious concept of ethical imagining. Ethical imagining implies a kind of social devotion somewhat analogous to ordinary baby care.

What ethical imagining does not need, however, is sentimentality or being nice.

49 *Wittgenstein, p 74*

In the relaxation that belongs to trust and to acceptance of the professional reliability (be it psychotherapeutic, social work, architectural, etc.), there is room for the idea of unrelated thought sequences which the analyst will do well to accept as such, not assuming the existence of a significant thread.[50]

And now another conundrum that I push into the foreground of ethical imagining: our social or our intrapsychic environment (or both) leaving "room for unrelated thought sequences, accepted as such," rather than inserting a demand for order and purpose. This is a model of a nexus in which one can consider what seems to be useless or destructive babble without correcting or condemning it. There is more at stake in an enclave of luxury than obstacles to one's opinions and purposes. And, to return to the paradox, there can be room for imaginings unrelated to shared illusory experiences of ethical practice. There can be room for incongruity, tangentiality, for any image or idea between non-sequitor and *primum non nocere*.

50 *Winnicott, p 65*

I am fiddling with the idea that ethical imagining is not *a priori* constrained by one's conscience or censored by one's guilt. Ethical imagining, as I am exploring it, is imagining where in a situation an ethics might be, not concluding what decisive action or thought to promote or avoid. Ethical imagining as I am exploring it is envisioning any situation as if there might be an ethical interpretation of it, and then pondering which details sparkle in the foreground as emanations of ethical clues. As I think writing and write thinking here, I know better than to take on the entire history of Western philosophical discourse upon what is to be done.

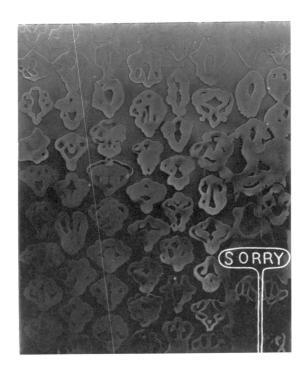

Graham Gilmore [b. Canada 1963]
Sorry (1st version), 1997
Oil and enamel on masonite panel, 76 x 61 cm
Collection of James Lahey
Courtesy of the artist and Monte Clark Gallery, Vancouver and Toronto

I am not emphasizing the value of useless or contradictory babble as a prelude to constructing a system, or even a situation where the illusory experience of free speech is shared. I am emphasizing a social nexus and also a personal psychological nexus in which there is safety, in spite of relaxation of the demands of the Technological Ethos and Freud's Reality Principle; there is safety without mental dependence upon traditional moral righteousness.

> It is only here, in this unintegrated state of the personality...that that which we describe as creative can appear. This, if reflected back, but only if reflected back, becomes part of the organized individual personality.[51]

The excessive confidence of the psychoanalytic tone ossifies this insight. I am rewriting it:

51 *Winnicott, p 75*

Only here, in this unintegrated state of conversation or contemplation... can that which we describe as creative appear. This, if reflected back, but only if reflected back, becomes part of the ethical body politic.

(Reflection in this sense means acknowledged, described, represented—not acted upon or performed literally.)

Wittgenstein wrote, "All is in flux. Perhaps this is the very place to start."[52]

In this context, I would rewrite also: "When anything is in flux, this is when to start ethical imagining."

Although a social setting in flux is easily depicted, it is also a possible depiction of one's own psychological moment. I question that enclaves of luxury are so fragile that they cannot withstand episodes of inconsistency and confusion. And I question the nervous silence that implies people in an enclave of luxury should fear acknowledging and honouring jumble *per se*. I question that in an enclave of luxury mere ideas can magically incite robbery and mayhem. Yet so many

---

52 *Wittgenstein, p 3*

attempts at disruption of expectations are met with anxiety and disdain. Individually and socially it seems a reflex, over-rewarded as we are in enclaves of luxury, to intervene wherever a mess is made, including the mess of morally idiotic speech. In 2004 in Quebec, CHOI radio, with its brutish misogynous and xenophobic language, lost its federal broadcast license. The body politic was in a quandary, unsure whether it could buffer or withstand such mean ideas. There was ample fear that hateful ideas inflame hatred; that they inflame property damage and bodily harm. It is as if everyone agrees with Freud. On a moment's notice *homo homini lupus*.

Yet I am not writing about free speech or government censor-ship: the relevance of this to ethical imagining is in the loss of equanimity that occurs when one's very own unspoken imaginings include lawlessness and cruelty.

It is not publicly acknowledged, certainly not celebrated that in one's own psyche moral uproariousness is a vital stage from which the form, the idea, the structure of ethical insight might emerge.

I am pondering whether people living in an enclave of luxury have the guts to recognize uproar, so familiar in play, as a vital stage from which the form, the idea, the structure of ethics might emerge.

Vernon Ah Kee [b. Australia 1967]
not an animal or a plant, 2005-2006
Vinyl lettering
Installation view, Museum | London, 2006
Photograph: Vernon Ah Kee
Courtesy of the artist and Bellas Milani Gallery, Brisbane

If I say I trust my own mind *primum non nocere*, this is non-sensical. I am my "mind" (plus the rest of me). And consciousness, if that's what I am referring to with the phrase "my mind," doesn't do anything, let alone harm or help; "mind" is a figment of subjectivity that may be inflamed or immured in enclaves of luxury; "mind" is experienced and practiced according to a multiplicity of definitions. Consciousness has no material product. But consciousness certainly is not worthless until it results in an action. To the extent I "trust" my own consciousness as it meanders, I am confident my own consciousness isn't vulnerable to impulsive willing. I could say I trust the process of playful imagining. This playfulness satisfies Aristotle's criterion for "good" because it is valuable as an end in itself. That it effects something else valuable is a surprise, not a purpose. This trustworthy playfulness *se invicem redant, se nihil acturos quod posit in alterius adnum cedere,* "makes one confident that [one's mind] can do nothing which will harm others." Whether others trust their own minds is their own affair, but if such trust is possible, then the ethics of a situation might reveal itself when imagining is actually released from moral truisms. What if there is no pre-established code that imagining must comply with?

If this willing suspension of guilt is possible, could the ethics of a situation finally, paradoxically, reveal itself? By this I mean, if a situation imagined to the extreme becomes "a virtual version that includes what isn't there and what might be there as well," could this imagining become so extreme that one's emotions could not be ignored? I am not speaking of rumination or fantasy as pleasures in themselves; for the realms of paranoia and ecstasy can be entirely familiar, depending on the community a person lives in. Contrasted to witnessing in this medium or that, contrasted with images in magazines, books, movies, paintings, television, the internet, etc. what if deliberate imaginary involvement is pushed far far beyond familiarity? What if this deliberate imagining led one to supercede the limits of one's own unexamined ethics? I am assuming a devotion to deliberate imagining pushed beyond (familial, communal and yes, even mass-) mediated limits, loosened far beyond twinge of conscience. This is where perhaps a visceral response would be ignited. This is the moment, the subjective phase, at which, viscerally, "perturbing and ethical become sisterly."

The enmeshment of personal consciousness, insofar as it is personal psychosomatic embodiment of an extreme imagined scene, just might usher an ethical interpretation into the foreground. I am distinguishing "the limit of one's ethics" as a matter of interpretation, not the self-imposition of, or intimidation by a moral code. This emergence of the idea of ethical is an interpretation, a provisional exploration, because of which one may consider much (not excluding one's decisions of course) even while not knowing what to do next.

I find it hard to believe that deliberate imagining of involvement, the evocation of imaginary details to extremes beyond familiarity, would make one less aware of ethics, or of one's own relations with other humans. How could this weaken one's capacity for interpretation? In enclaves of luxury what time and money, energy, or consciousness will be wasted by ethical imagining as I have described it?

Does material luxury matter so much that imagining *per se* threatens it?

Walter Tandy Murch [b. Canada 1907, d. United States 1967]
Pressure Gauge, c. 1965
Graphite on paper, 70.5 x 54 cm
Private Collection. With permission of the artist's estate

Ethical imagining of this kind imbues anything we please
with the awareness of an ethical background, a background
that is a perturbation of the foreground of consciousness
grown tepid in moral truisms. Or, I am tempted to say, scorched
in a firestorm of commodities and images of commodities.

Even while I know imagining needn't, for better and for worse,
lead to just doing it (whatever *it* turns out to be), at some
point humans in enclaves of desperation will insist we
acknowledge their situation with our deeds. Ethical imagining
is not hopeless as the background, the ambience (rather than
the exception prior to) ethical action. As vapourous as ethical
imagining is, it is a privilege. There can be an ethics of luxury.
In our enclaves of luxury, we could be the very ones to enjoy
the luxury of ethics.

And in over-rewarded enclaves there can be the luxury of
ethics. As vapourous as it is, it can be a perturbation that
re-interprets the enclave of luxury we live in so naturally.

It is not publicly acknowledged, certainly not celebrated, that in one's own psyche moral uproariousness is a vital stage from which the form, the idea, the structure of ethical insight might emerge.

I am pondering whether people living in an enclave of luxury have the guts to recognize uproar, so familiar in play, as a plentiful stage from which the form, the idea, the structure of ethics might emerge.

I have said all of this without any capacity to decide what should happen in the case of radio CHOI. I have said all of this without knowing whether it matters to distinguish an ethics of scarcity from an ethics of luxury; whether it matters that one develops an ethics of trust in addition to Freud's "ethics" of self defense.

Dostoyevsky, if I recall correctly, was of the opinion that the human tragedy consists in our being able to adapt to anything. It would seem to me that this is the ethical challenge not only for those who care for babies, but for those who care period. It is a widely shared adult illusory experience that we are "able to take care of ourselves." This can be imposed too literally. Existential consciousness of one's dependence is not "only for the feeble." I am saying this in recognition of our absolute dependence on each other for what is meaningful, for what has value, and for whatever contributes to making sense of life.

In enclaves of luxury would there not be nourishment of these so-called meanings, values and sense? The latter ideas, "meanings, values, sense" are familiar, almost too familiar. They are just what I mean by "illusory experiences" so thoughtlessly taken for granted. As communally shared states of mind, we assume meanings, values and sense to be readily available. It seems natural rather than wondrous that these ignite a transformative process: transforming objects and events into culture.

In using the word culture I am thinking of the inherited tradition. I am thinking of something that is in the common pool of humanity, into which individuals and groups of people may contribute, and from which we may all draw if we have somewhere to put what we find.[53]

"Somewhere to put what we find" is a vague statement, so ambiguous it is almost a verbal Rorschach test. This "somewhere" is an illusion with ethical dimensions.

There is no "somewhere" literally in the brain. This "somewhere" is an illusory experience. To say there is a "somewhere" is my way of dramatizing illusory experience as valuable or not according to the community's joy to sustain it. Pondering this "somewhere" I conceive of it as a person's remembered context. It refers to knowledge, memories, longings, and judgments into which we immerse what we draw from "the cultural pool." This "somewhere" could be described as the psyche's counterpart to a social nexus. Or it could be the psyche's impression of how a present moment, the experience rummaged from the "cultural pool" and the past are connected. It could be "room" that Spinoza called for, room in which to reason well and to doubt. "Somewhere" is a metaphor, as is "room."

53 *Winnicott, p 116*

Maybe this "somewhere" is a virtual revision of something objectively perceived as well as subjectively experienced in the cultural pool.

Could it be that the "somewhere to put what we find" is none other than "the playing process" of consciousness?

If this "somewhere" is a mental landscape, the ethical challenge is to honour it as, metaphorically, an aspect of the biosphere, instead of a landfill site, a tar sands, the world's biggest billboard.

Metaphors of landfill sites, tar sands and billboards lead to the question whether there is such an action as exploiting psyches or colonizing consciousness. Immanuel Kant has already advised us to

> So act as to treat humanity, whether in thine own person or in that of any other, in every case as an end, never as a means only.[54]

54 *Immanuel Kant,* The Metaphysical Elements of Ethics, *(1780), trans. Thomas Kingsmill Abbott, http://www.infomotions.com/etexts/philosophy/ 1700-1799/kant-metaphysical-145.txt*

In enclaves of luxury, superficially, one's neighbour is one's fellow. The economic life in enclaves of luxury, however, is based to some extent on commercial institutions whose modus operandi is using persons as a means. This is to say that their work and their psyches are objects, objects to be moved (in all senses of that word). Objectifying psyches reduces people to a function in the service of an agenda. One may be cautioned not to "treat humanity" like an object, like the means to an agenda. All I am contemplating in this essay is the possibility at least of not thinking of—imagining—one's neighbour as an object in an agenda, or, more to the point, no thoughtless acceptance of other persons as the objects of some plan or purpose.

There must be such a thing as respecting the "somewhere" in life or in psyche, not because it is real estate to which each person has legal title, but because objectifying it objectifies a person.

There will always be someone—or institutions—who can give reasons why objectifying psyches is necessary in enclaves of luxury. And, as I said, in enclaves of luxury we can afford to listen to their reasons and converse about them.

A template upon which ethical social relations could be elaborated seems possible. Although I have proffered a template from the nurturer-infant relationship, my concluding reflections do not invoke apple pie.

This baby-parent relationship is about as inherently ethical as humans get. Not that it doesn't, as a template, need revisions galore to acquire relevance to adult life, but as a template it is evocative, which might just be as good a beginning as any. I am not beefing up this model to serve as the basis of a legal system, or of an ideal society, or as an atheist version of "The Sermon on the Mount."

We may consider much, while not knowing what to do next.

If there is the possibility of an ethics of luxury, the genesis of it surely would include ethical imagining, which is to say playfulness in between the extremes of sadism and empathy—along with whatever else. This long-winded consideration of trust, flux, play and intrapsychic landscape is my way of triangulating toward ethical imagining as a group observance. As I mentioned,

> If people value camaraderie in ethical circumstances, then they will represent these circumstances (explicitly and/or implicitly) with artfulness; there will be reciprocity between circumstances and imagination. An ethical imagination will ripen.

We have the medium of conversation in which to do the same.

Yes, I do know the hypothesis of ethical imagining in enclaves
of luxury now shows itself as a familiar paradox:

What is objectively perceived [such as ethical conditions] is by
definition to some extent subjectively conceived of [perhaps
by ethical imagining].[55]

There is no resolving the paradox. For the pragmatist, this
paradox is more than unresolved: it could be the muddy cliff
upon which these reflections, none too waterproof, appear
to actually welcome rain.

55 *Winnicott, p 77*

Ryan Arnott
Untitled (Diamond), 1992 (detail)
Acrylic, graphite, colour pencil, conté on paper, 56.0 x 76.0 cm
Collection of the Art Gallery of Hamilton
Courtesy of the artist

IHOR HOLUBIZKY

AFTERWORD

To say that the meaning of luxury has undergone a change is an understatement: butter, as my stepmother told me, was a luxury for everyone in war-time England; matches, as my father told me, were a luxury in western Ukraine before the war. In today's culture and society it has its own matrix (no cinematic pun intended) of paradoxes and contradiction. In the pre-industrial age, luxury was for the few, an indulgence and sumptuous self-pampering. The means were inherited more than earned—and therefore rarely questioned. Everyone knew their place—especially the privileged dandy who could lay waste to the family fortune in the pursuit of leisure. The nouveau riche of the 19th century industrial age were, in sharp contrast, self-made. They could punch their way through social class barriers by embracing signs of luxury—the accumulation of material wealth—and thus establishing their presence.

In turn they provided the means and opportunity for a new strata of society—the middle class—to achieve their own levels of luxury—what we can now call materialism. But the nouveau riche could also have an altruistic side in their relationship to the masses and the poor. Andrew Carnegie espoused the moral obligation of the wealthy to give their fortunes away (and authored *The Gospel of Wealth* in 1889).

After selling his steel company et.al. to J.P Morgan for $480 million in 1911 (a vast sum 100 years ago), he set up the Carnegie Corporation of New York. a philanthropic foundation. One of the initiatives was the funding of libraries—more than 2500 throughout the English-speaking world. But the libraries were only a delivery system. It spoke as much of a moral rectitude characteristic of the late Victorian age; the lessons of a Scottish Presbyterian background were not lost on Carnegie. He declared, "Only in popular education can man erect the structure of an enduring civilization." It is doubtful that this "enduring civilization" meant anything but the world order as he saw it.

Ethics—as a philosophical necessity—was rarely in the equation because it has/had no materialistic component. All this has bubbled and popped over the past century—war was good for business, and depressions were good for the accumulation of wealth (feeding on misery).

To extrapolate from Jeanne Randolph's commentaries, it is as good a time as any to ask questions and not simply to continue berating materialism and demonizing its adherents. As she notes, we in the West—the Old World, the New World and Other (British postcolonial) Worlds—all belong to a privileged enclave.

To lean on a comment made by American painter Ad Reinhardt in 1966—materialism is neither good nor bad for people, but anyone looking to it for salvation will be sorely disappointed.

Luxury is not materialism but has been bonded as if a genetic matter to consumerism. Indeed art has become one of the consumables. So how bad can materialism be if it serves culture and cultural producers who, ironically, may be delivering the opposite message in their work. In this way, and others, luxury is linked to taste ... not merely the objectification of preference as a philosophical game, but a skill to be honed, sharpened, and used like a rapier. Vulgarity, "inevitably," is the thrust and parry.

The captains of merchandising—a subset of the captains of industry—have told us that towels of a certain weight and quality are luxurious, and in turn, toilet paper of a certain quality is also luxurious. Luxurious therefore, is a relative term to an ever-expanding sphere of what-luxury-is—what we need—what we aspire to. Many doors must be passed through—a code must be learned—the game is the game. So why stumble over toilet paper?

It is a question of ethics—not a moralistic position against luxury —nor to prove or disprove that Money Creates Taste, a *bon mot* from American artist Jenny Holzer.

My commentary has a personal perspective, affording myself this "luxury" to establish my own relationship to Jeanne Randolph's writing and thoughts, as every reader can and must with reasoning and imagination. [Twenty-three years ago I titled a self-penned song-monologue, *The Age of Reason(able) Pleasure*. Little did I know.]

Like Jeanne, I've lived in many cities around the world, each adding to my sense of place-and-being. It is no one place, and perhaps this deforms my sense of being, comfort becoming discomfort. Over the past 18 months I found my relationship to (and understanding of) materialism destabilized. Whatever I owned and valued is either gone by circumstances or no longer has the value that I once attached to it. I still desire things—it is a second nature—but with no fixed address, how much do I really need? By the same token I can take my imagination—my intellectual property—anywhere. That is to say, I know/and believe that I DO have intellectual property, which is not "held within" things. This too is a privileged position—my own piece-of-the-enclave.

Station A:
Staying at M and T's house, January 2007.

The house is located in a highly desirable neighbourhood: the neighbours are the moneyed class, which is not to say that M and T are "one" (or "two") of them. They made a decision to live there many years ago and their "position" was hard-fought. The house was in the final stages of renovations — modest in comparison to what is going on elsewhere — a modernist extension yet keeping the character of the original house. The new spaces have been designed with attention to detail (aesthetics in all of its fullness) — and rooms that did not need a "make-over" have been left alone (another decision).

Everything is carefully considered — not for its own sake, but for the sake of living. It is an expression of the art of living, a phrase used by T, not for them alone, but the idea that the art of living has a particularness and does not come with an absolute measure (keeping up with the Joneses). Design comes with a financial and psychological price, as anyone who has gone through a domestic renovation will know.

At one stage the house was unliveable. M and T have camped out in temporary bedrooms and used temporary kitchens over two years. It is nearing an end, almost miraculously. With this finish line in view, M expressed a pent-up exasperation, the state of not-having. As soon as it was uttered in my presence, the comment was caught in the air: there was an apology, but none was needed. I did not take the comment as being insensitive, and knew she meant what we call "creature comforts."

Other close friends, who do mean well, have offered the thought that it must be a (my) blessing to have no material burdens, as if a Zen-like state. I know this not to be true because I still live in a material world. Or, *if* it were a Zen-state, it is neither good nor bad... but simply the way it is.

The next day I posed a related question to T, who then spoke of credit-driven luxury and its inevitable trap, a form of indentured servitude to greed. T also spoke of the counter-scenario—a friend whose "worth" goes up and down, but who understands and practices the art of living. It is living within means and knowing how to appreciate the circumstances, whereas debt-bound "luxuriators" can never see an art in not-having.

The art of living cannot be to literally "savour every moment as if it were the last." Otherwise we would be paralyzed in a string of morbid moments because the last is the end. It would snuff out imagination and hope for the future.

M and T's house is designed for living rather than a monument to materialism and their productive lives as artists keep things in check.

"Ah—ha!" you say... "They're artists... no wonder."

Being an artist is to understand what is humbling—a position in the food chain that is always, at best, tenuous. (Neither is it a key to the kingdom of taste.) If the demon of luxury is materialism—as the demon of modern is modernism—it brings us to the notion of the affluent society, and to be specific, John Kenneth Galbraith's examination of American society of the 1950s (a "Canadian spanner in the works?"). At risk of over-simplification, he saw an American society that was rich in the private sector but poor in the public sector (his original book title was the pedantic *Why the Poor are Poor*). The have and have-not scenario had an infrastructural solution—Galbraith saw a need for better public education, medical care, roads, and so on. (How different is this from Andrew Carnegie's assertion?) At the same time, he recognized that a desire for useless things was being generated through advertising—"luxury goods" for the ever-growing leisure class, no longer a clearly defined middle class. The Democratic Party (the ruling class) embraced Galbraith's views with a War on Poverty. But that is true to the American form—the war on tyranny (War of Independence), the war on drugs, the war on terrorism...

In the "wake" of Galbraith's *Affluent Society*, professor Donald Horne authored a book on Australian society. Its title *The Lucky Country* became the *de facto* national mantra:

> In a hot summer's night in December 1964 I was about to write the last chapter of a book on Australia. The opening sentence of this last chapter was: "Australia is a lucky country, run by second-rate people who share its luck."[1]

---

1 *Donald Horne*. The Lucky Country: Australia in the Sixties (*Melbourne: Penguin, 1966) p 217*

As any thinking Australian will know, it is a brutal indictment of the ways things were—and perhaps still are. At the time of Horne's book, Australian aborigines were still "non-people," not yet "lucky" enough to join the nation-club. In Horne's view Australian affluence was lazy and indifferent.

There is more than a passing relationship between our age of affluence and materialism and Machiavelli's dictum, in *The Prince*, penned in 1513: "men forget the death of a father more quickly than the loss of a patrimony." In contemporary terms, killing, genocide, indifference to human rights, etc. are more easily "reconciled" than the loss of land or property. The unthinkable is troublesome—our affluence has a demon side. Thinking about the unthinkable and ethics is an on-going conversation with T, and the impossibility of seeing traces— as Jeanne Randolph has noted—as Scottish philosopher David Hume questioned causation (causality) more than 260 years ago: "We cannot penetrate into the reason of the conjunction. We only observe the thing itself, and always find that from the constant conjunction the objects acquire a union in the imagination."[2] The answer (as immutable reality?) is not so easily found, nor "blowing in the wind." Or is it?

2 A Treatise of Human Nature (1740) (Charlston SC: Biblio Bazaar, 2006) p 103

Station B (halfway round the world):
Staying at R and F's house, February 2007.

R is an artist—F is an architect. Not more of the same, but a comparable distinction. Their house is a practical solution, renovated and expanded over time with recycled materials that informed decisions. It is not a patchwork but neither is it a pristine modernism. Although close to the city centre, the house sits on a high prospect (very desirable) overlooking bushland. There are ample spaces designed for living/lounging/pondering—a subtropical luxury. The back of the house opens up and is kept open for most of the year. This is more than a view to nature—"it" will come in—ants to the table and to a laptop as well as feral peacocks to the door. What more a sign of old luxury could you imagine? It took me aback... dare I shoo-away a peacock?

Twixt Stations A and B:
The smoker's lounge in the transit zone of Narita Airport.

The lounge is newly designed with an Alphaville-coolness. I sat watching a multi-projector display that occupied two entire walls, moving through a corner. Images of nature flowed past, with moving text. A haiku sequence read:

The sea in the evening
Smooth as a pond
And my smoke
Like a Matisse painting

Was it art? I am enough of an "interrogator" to have spotted the Winston logo elsewhere in the "display," but who's to say that others didn't—and "knew." I could have struck up a conversation, but to what end? To debate the smokiness of Matisse or whether Manet was the first to depict a cigarette in a painting in 1863? We would all come to our own conclusions, and for that moment it was enough to indulge in the luxury of a last refuge.

I have my laptop—iTunes are loaded should I need a mood inducement. There are books of use to me—to feed my intellectual hunger—anywhere I go. And if all else fails, there are worlds to imagine.

Regarding Consumption

When I imagine consumption—whether in a conceptual, allegorical, political, economic, or social sense—I see visceral, salivary and awesome spectral images. These images form an imaginary film montage as I process the thoughts inspired by this book on ethics, materialism and abundance. Jeanne Randolph contextualizes the materialization of fantasies (the Bomb, plastics, television, computers, antibiotics, etc.) around the location of public unreason: advertising and the cold war realization that our entire world could actually explode. For Georges Bataille [1897-1962] there was a surplus of energy on the globe that exceeded what was strictly necessary for maintaining human life. His concept of the "accursed share," was the surplus energy that any system, natural or cultural, must expend; and according to Bataille, the way in which each society dealt with material excess most clearly defined that society: "...if the excess cannot be completely absorbed in its growth, it must necessarily be lost without profit; it must be spent, willingly or not, gloriously or catastrophically."[1] This text is striking (as is the volume you are holding) in the way it contrasts with conventional economic models of scarcity and utility. For Bataille, luxury was the contrary of necessity; luxury presents humans with their fundamental problems. Homer Simpson [circa 1987] analogously called beer the cause

1   *Georges Bataille,* The Accursed Share: An Essay on General Economy, *trans. Robert Hurley, (New York, Zone Books, 1988) p 21*

of, and solution to, all our problems. Homer embodies an iconic figure of unproductive labour in contemporary Western society. In his famous daydream "The Land of Chocolate," the streets are made of chocolate, as are the lampposts and a dog which he chomps on. This vision of excess and leisure may be traced in art to the medieval land of Cockaigne, a land of plenty where the harshness of peasant life does not exist. Pieter Bruegel the Elder painted this in 1567. There was a 13th century poem entitled *The Land of Cockaigne* and the etymology of Cockaigne is French, derived from a word for a small sweet cake. In my montage, cakes, sweetness and eating predominate, accompanied by the song "Big Rock Candy Mountain" written by Harry McClintock in 1928. The lyrics describe cigarette trees and lakes of alcohol; in the children's version of the song there are lakes of soda pop and streams of lemonade. Things a homeless person might fear are rendered harmless—the dogs have rubber teeth, and police have wooden legs. This song was used by Burger King™ in 1985, with the words changed to sell Tender-Crisps™, a chicken sandwich. My imaginary montage lazily dissolves into the scene from the film *Willy Wonka and the Chocolate Factory* (1971) where the protagonists ride a contraption like Santa's sled through oozing marshmallow foam. This segues to Sesame Street's Cookie Monster (circa 1971) eating donuts, letters, a computer, anything really. Pica is an appetite for earth and other non-foods. Geophagia, the act of eating mud, is a centuries old practice, but in contemporary clinical practice often considered an eating disorder. Yet it occupies a place between nourishment and waste. This omnivorous capacity may be turned into a radical gesture, as byartist Rita McKeough in her performance *Take it to the Teeth* (1993) in which she masticates the walls of a museum. This implied consumption—tasting, tearing and regurgitating the walls—draws ideas of excess, waste, and landfill into a space of institutional critique. Institutions and the structures that frame society—government, religion and architecture, for example—encourage particular practices and economies of consumption. During the cold war, dreams of excess formed a consensual nightmare of nuclear power and the spectral image of atoms ceaselessly multiplying in a chain reaction—a surplus energy that would not be contained—as seen in Hiroshima, or in Chernobyl. Atomic visions seemed more palpable then, more commonly circulating in the media's representation of cold war politics. While these possibilities have not disappeared, their circulation in the media has diminished. This shows how illusions and reality are consensual, how they are a shared and cultural construction created collectively. In *Ethics of Luxury*, Jeanne encourages us all to imagine: "Imagining takes place in a zone of experience across which it becomes gradually indistinguishable from art...art elaborates what isn't there and elaborates what could be there; this is the way art toys with what a society has already recognized consensually as basically 'real.'"

ANTHONY KIENDL
DIRECTOR, PLUG IN ICA, WINNIPEG

*A*CKNOWLEGMENTS

This book would not ever have come to fruition without
Anthony Kiendl's steadfastness. Anthony not only provided
three months' residency at The Dunlop Art Gallery critic-in-
residence program and ushered me into a Paul D. Fleck
Fellowship for an Independent Residency at The Banff Centre,
but he then championed this book on behalf of Plug In ICA
in Winnipeg. He also bestowed upon me his personal jolly
encouragement. I will always be indebted to YYZBOOKS
publication committee past and present, a commitment that
has lasted sixteen years, this time around with editor Robert
Labossiere. Robert provided what mattered so much to me,
as it would to all writers, an invitation to show him a draft
of whatever I was working on; he followed through with
administrative devotion and perfect editorial insight when I
needed it most. This is the second book that Susan Chafe has
designed with all her creativity and graceful humour. She is a
true comrade—like my other persevering buddy, Ihor Holubizky,
whose Afterword is worth reading at least four times and
thinking about for several years. Everything I ever think or
write is suffused with the love and insight of Bernie Miller
and Sigrid Dahle.

JEANNE RANDOLPH